T0165036

THE

DANGER OF PLAYING
HIDE AND SEEK

The Problem of Playing a Childhood
Game in Your Daily Walk with God

Terri Leigh Cox

With a Foreword by
Judy Jacobs

WestBow
P R E S S
A DIVISION OF THOMAS NELSON

WestBow Press books may be ordered through booksellers or by contacting:

WestBow Press
A Division of Thomas Nelson
1663 Liberty Drive
Bloomington, IN 47403
www.westbowpress.com
1-(866) 928-1240

Because of the dynamic nature of the Internet, any web addresses or
links contained in this book may have changed since publication and
may no longer be valid. The views expressed in this work are solely those
of the author and do not necessarily reflect the views of the publisher,
and the publisher hereby disclaims any responsibility for them.

Any people depicted in stock imagery provided by Thinkstock are
models, and such images are being used for illustrative purposes only.

Certain stock imagery © Thinkstock.

ISBN: 978-1-4497-3710-8 (sc)
ISBN: 978-1-4497-3711-5 (hc)
ISBN: 978-1-4497-3709-2 (e)
Library of Congress Control Number: 2012900665

Printed in the United States of America

WestBow Press rev. date: 02/16/2012

THE DANGER OF PLAYING
HIDE-AND-SEEK

"I could ask the darkness to hide me and the light
around me to become night—
but even in darkness I cannot hide from You!"

Psalm 139:11-12
New Living Translation

Contents

Dedication

I dedicate this book to my spiritual mentors that God has placed in my life for such a time as this—Kathy Hagerman, Pastor Judy Jacobs-Tuttle, and Dr. Angela St. John.

I gave my heart to the Lord at the age of thirteen, and I did not even know what the term "mentor" meant, much less what it meant to have one in your life. On that day when I gave my heart to the Lord, I began a journey that would lead me to where I am today. God has brought these three strong women of the faith into my life to lead, guide, and teach me the things that He desires for me to know about the ministry, about His heart, about my destiny, and about myself.

<u>Kathy Hagerman</u>: When our paths crossed, I don't think either one of us realized where that moment would lead us. I have absolutely no regrets whatsoever. We have been through so much together, and that is the key—we've gone through it … and made it to the mountaintop! You have allowed me to walk beside you in ministry, and you gave me wings to fly. You were the first person to truly "hear" the song in my heart and spirit, and when life got too hard and I wanted to quit, you sang my song back to me when I forgot the words. You've always pointed me to Jesus, no matter what I was facing, and encouraged me to keep pressing on, because in the end it will be worth it all. You have truly been my "other mother." I love you—"just because!"

<u>Pastor Judy Jacobs Tuttle</u>: Three years ago, I stepped foot on the campus of the International Institute of Mentoring for the first time, and my life has never been the same since that day. So first, I must say "thank you" for your obedience to the call of God on your life. Without your obedience, my life would not be, my life would not be headed in the direction that it is today. God has used you to help bring me out of my "hiding places" and into new places of freedom. Because of your love, ongoing

encouragement, support, and never-ending prayers, I am daring to dream again, and I am seeing what I am speaking start to unfold right before my very eyes. Through the darkest times of this past year, you have been there—and from the depths of my heart, I say "thank you." I am so glad that we are on this journey together. I am honored to call you my pastor, my mentor, and my friend. Love, love, love you.

Dr. Angela St. John: Where do I begin? Well, we all know that it all truly began with a "hammer and a stone." Hard to believe that we have only known each other for three years, because it seems like we have known each other forever. At times you can speak to me exactly what I am thinking before I can even say it. You can finish my sentences, and sometimes without me saying a thing, you know when I just need to hear a familiar voice. In those moments you pick up the phone or send a text if you are pressed for time. The words that God gives to you are so "on-time" and right on target for that moment, because He never misses; but He has to have a willing heart that will allow Him to use them to be His mouthpiece. God has used you to not only bring spiritual healing to my life but also physical and emotional healing. You are truly my "sister of the heart, from the very start." Look how far we've come, and we've only scratched the surface. Can't wait to see what all He has in store … those things we "know not of." Love you so much.

I dedicate this book last and surely not least to my Lord and Savior, Jesus Christ. Without Him, this book would never have been possible. I am so humbled that He would allow me to write "His" book, and pen my name to it as the author. As the old song goes, "Without Him, I cold do nothing, and without Him, I'd surely fail." It is my prayer that each person who reads this book will be touched in the very core of their being by the spirit of God and will be brought closer to His heart. I am so thankful to be able to write this book for His glory and to share His heart through my own life, so that others may know and "be blessed."

Foreword

In her book, *The Danger of Playing Hide-and-Seek,*
Terri paints a vivid portrait of the position that she
found herself in after many years of challenges, both
physical, emotional, and especially spiritual.

The playfulness of hide-and-seek is always a fun
game to play if you are a toddler, a preschooler, or
maybe even a middle-schooler, but there comes a
time in our lives when, as the writer of Hebrews
tells us:

> For though by this time you ought to be
> teachers, you need someone to teach you again
> the *first principles* of the oracles of God; and
> you have come to need milk and not solid
> food. For everyone who partakes only of milk
> is *unskilled* in the world of righteousness, for he

is a *babe;* But sold food belongs to those who *are full of age,* that is, those who by reason of use have their senses exercised to discern both good and evil. (Hebrews 5:12-14)

I believe as you read this book you are going to be encouraged by this strong woman of faith to *stop* the games and go on to higher heights and deeper depths in God to become all that He has positioned and purposed you to become through Jesus Christ our Lord and Savior. It is my prayer that as you read this book, you will understand, as Jeremiah 29:11 declares:

> For I know the plans that I have for you, saith the Lord, plans to prosper you and to give you a future and a hope.

Come on out of hiding, because now you have been found by Him . . . *you are "it."*

Judy Jacobs Tuttle
Pastor, Mentor, Author, Psalmist
Cleveland, Tennessee

Endorsements

I am filled with the joy of the Lord, seeing my "spiritual daughter" living in the gift that our Lord Jesus Christ has given her. Not being moved by circumstances from the past, present, or future; but daily walking in His joy.

Terri is one of the most gifted writers, because she is led by God's Holy Spirit. In 2006, she was with me in a revival that I was invited to come and speak at. Before going to the podium, I told her to pick up a pen and write what the Holy Spirit gave to her as she listened to the words I was speaking. After I spoke, she handed me what she had written, and it was as if the Holy Ghost had given out a prophetic word. When I read it to the congregation, it was anointed, and it confirmed the word that had been preached.

In this book, you will find that same anointing that she walks in—using her own life as an example to teach the way of the Lord, and to help others come out of "hiding" and to live in the light of His Word.

Rev. Kathy Hagerman
Co-Pastor of Living Water Fellowship
Bluefield, West Virginia

If I knew then what I know now about the game of hide-and-seek, I would have come out from hiding a long time ago. In this book, Terri uncovers the dangers of hiding in places you think you can't be found in order to save your life, only to find out that it is to your own detriment. Stepping out "from behind the tree" of self-sabotage and false identities and exposing yourself to the real "finder," Jesus Christ, is the only way to "tag" your true freedom.

Dr. Angela St. John
Chiropractic Physician
Cleveland, Tennessee

After reading *The Danger of Playing Hide-and-Seek,* one is assured of God's faithfulness and His divine plan for our lives. As you read this book, you begin a journey, and as the text unfolds, you realize that in many ways we are all traveling down the same path. God is calling His people to a place of maturity and leaving behind childish games of our past. This book will enrich your fellowship with God and deepen your understanding of His nature.

Pastor Andrew Towe
Lead Pastor, Power Plant Ministry Center
Chattanooga, Tennessee

In reading this book you truly get the essence of who Terri Cox is and the message that she is a wonderful, tender-hearted person. I want to recommend this book as good reading for wisdom being given bundled up in a nice cover, wrapped in a passion for God, displaying nuggets of freedom for all to have. Hide-and-seek refers to a game we all have played, but God wants us to run straight to Him, because we know He already knows where we are. That is why as Terri would say, "There is true freedom in being found by the Seeker." Enjoy your read, and know that God will take you to His hiding place.

Minister Chris Allen
Worship Leader, Songwriter, Producer
Cleveland, Tennessee

In *The Danger of Playing Hide-and-Seek,* Terri encourages us to come out of hiding and into the purpose God created in each of us. By exposing lies of the enemy that lead to complacency, she challenges us to grab hold of destiny tightly, and pursue God passionately. Terri's story offers encouragement through her personal examples of how to endure hardships, confront challenges, and overcome obstacles to see our dreams come true.

Dr. Sheila Cornea
Dean of International Institute of Mentoring
Inspirational Communicator & Coach
Gutsy Grace Resources
Cleveland, Tennessee

Introduction

Have you ever played the childhood game called hide-and-seek? Most of us have played this game at least once in our lives—whether it was while we were growing up as children, raising our own children, or perhaps while you were babysitting children for friends. No matter what the circumstance, we are all familiar with this game. Have you ever stopped to think that maybe you might be playing this same childhood game of hide-and-seek in your relationship with God?

As children, we learned from our parents how to play hide-and-seek. As we grew older, we may have carried these same learned traits into our spiritual walk with God. Were there times in your life when someone asked you to step out and do something out of your comfort zone, but because of fear and intimidation, you wouldn't take on that kind of responsibility?

Maybe you have a dream deep down inside your heart that you really want. Because of people telling you that you aren't good enough, that no one will ever listen to someone like you, or that you shouldn't believe you can do that, you never reach out for that dream.

Did you have people in your life who controlled you, kept you from reaching out and being all you knew you could be? So now you are just comfortable where you are, sitting on your pew, letting others be and do what you know you are called to do. Do you know why we do these things? We do them because of past hurts, circumstances, and things that we have gone through. We go into spiritual hiding—to try to protect ourselves from further hurt or injury, pain or rejection.

What we don't realize is that we are "hiding" from the true "seeker" and not allowing Him to bring us out of these "hiding places." We are setting ourselves up to miss out on the true freedom that is waiting for us when we reach the destiny God has chosen for our lives. You see, there is true freedom in being found by the Seeker.

Are you tired of hiding behind excuses and hiding in places that you think are keeping you safe? I know I am, and I believe I am hearing the heart of God calling out to His people, saying, "Ready or not, here I come."

So if you are hearing this too, then read on. I believe I hear Him saying to you, "Come out, come out, wherever you are."

Learned Behaviors

For the first nine months of living and working in Cleveland, Tennessee, I've been blessed to do private-duty nursing with a precious eight-year-old boy in the community I reside in. I have worked in the medical field since 2001 as a licensed practical nurse, and honestly I had never worked in pediatrics until I moved to Tennessee. I purposefully never took an assignment with pediatrics, because I never wanted to work with children. The only children I had ever really worked with were my nieces and nephews at home, and of course, there were all the children who grew up in the church; but I never had to deal with them in a medical capacity.

When I moved to Tennessee in December 2010, I began doing private-duty nursing. The first case

I was handed was a pediatric case, and I was not happy. Looking back over the past months that I have been his nurse, I have learned so much from him that I never would have learned had I not been given him as my first case. There is a Scripture in the Bible that talks about "iron sharpening iron" (Proverbs 27:17), and I have seen where I have not only been able to teach him as his nurse, but he has taught me so much about taking care of an eight-year-old. Sometimes I believe God has used him to help prepare me for my own children in the future. We never know what things God will use to prepare us for the next stages of our lives.

In nursing, we are taught that babies, toddlers, and elementary-age children are the most impressionable because they learn from what they see, hear, and experience. I see this a lot in working with my little eight-year-old. When he wakes up in the morning, he can be in the best mood ever; but let something go wrong in his schedule for the day or let someone around him be in a bad mood—his whole mood and attitude changes, and the whole day seems to be messed up. Now, he and I have certain times where we are working on things that benefit him, such as learning colors, shapes, numbers, and even walking in his gait trainer.

If I don't work with him, his parents, siblings, and other family members don't work with him, or his teachers in school don't work with him, he will never learn those shapes, colors, and numbers or how to position himself correctly in his gait trainer. When he does these things correctly, he is praised for his efforts; when they aren't done correctly, he isn't scolded but corrected in the right way, to see if he can perform the right action when asked again. The same thing occurs with the game hide-and-seek or peek-a-boo. Both of these childhood games are harmless, not meant to hurt anyone but to bring simple pleasure and entertainment. Isn't that what the enemy does with anything that God creates for His children? Think about it.

Our parents taught us how to play hide-and-seek as kids, how to choose a great hiding place that would keep us from the person who was looking for us until we could escape to safety—to home base. As adults, we have gone through trials and tests; we've been hurt and rejected; we are scared and intimidated, and the list goes on and on. So because of the learned behavior of knowing how to hide, we choose our hiding places carefully or we choose what thing we will hide behind so that we won't be hurt or rejected again.

All the time we are hiding, we think that we are being protected; but what we don't realize is that we are just playing hide-and-seek. God is waiting for us to play His version of the game, called "seek Me and be found." Sometimes we have to get so desperate in our search for God that we are willing to do whatever it takes to get what He has for us. In a song that Michael W. Smith sings called "Breathe," there is a line that says, "and I'm desperate for you." The truth is that just as we are desperate for Him, He is just as desperate for us. He wants to come and find us. He longs to spend time with His creation. We are the apple of His eye, and we are His beloved. Are you desperate enough to do whatever it takes to be brought out of your secret hiding places by the "true seeker" of your soul into your destiny and purpose?

Choosing Our Hiding Places

Think about our military men and women for a few minutes if you will.

When they are going out to battle or they are sneaking in for an attack and they have to hide, what are the characteristics of the places they might choose to hide or of something they might hide behind?

If you chose to hide somewhere or behind something, you want it to be a place that will protect you and keep you safe from harm. It should be someplace or something that will still allow you to see an oncoming attack from any outside source, and it should shelter you from any kind of storm that might come your way, right? Doesn't that sound like a place you might hide?

Looking back in my own life, there have been times certain emotions and feelings would emerge because of situations I would be facing, and thinking that it was my "right" to feel that way—would "hide" behind those emotions as a means of protecting me from further harm, rejection, etc. In reality, they were causing more damage and more harm than I realized. While I was hiding behind those emotions and feelings, I became so blinded to the enemy and what he was doing in my life at that moment. I couldn't see any oncoming attacks. As for shelter from the storm that I was facing at that time, there wasn't any at all. My hiding place provided no sense of security or safety.

You might be asking, "What kind of places did you choose to hide in?" For a long time, I hid in places called insecurity, low self-esteem, depression, intimidation, fear, approval addiction, and the culture of my familiar comfort zones from my childhood. You see, what I never truly realized is that the *only* place we should ever hide is in Jesus Christ.

"Hide me in the shadow of Your Wings."
Psalm 17:8b (NLT)

"For You are my hiding place; You protect me from trouble. You surround me with songs of victory."

Psalm 32:7 (NLT)

Jesus Christ provides us with all the protection and shelter we need from the attacks from the enemy. Now, that doesn't mean troubles won't come and that life will be simple or without trials and tests—by no means. There can be no testimony without a *test*.

When we start hiding in these places (sometimes also known as comfort zones), we are actually keeping ourselves in bondage and from moving on toward the next step that God has for our destiny. I know I had become so uncomfortable in who I was at that time in my life that I honestly could never see myself moving past where I existed. God loves us as we are, but He loves us enough to challenge us to always better ourselves. He wants us to be active, just like He is, and not passive. So let's be active in exploring some of those hiding places and those things that we sometimes hide behind, in order to be found by the Seeker and step into the freedom that awaits us all.

If we look in 1 Samuel 21:10-14, we see David fleeing to Gath, where he meets up with King Achish.

Many were not comfortable with him being there, and David was afraid of what this king might do to him. So what did he do? He pretended to be insane so that he would avoid any kind of confrontation or attack. Have you ever been so afraid of what someone would say or do to you that you came up with a plan that would make them not want to be around you or have anything to do with you? Sometimes I think that we look at people in the Bible and think that they are these super-spiritual people who really didn't face things like you or I face today. But I have come to realize more and more that even back then, God chose to use plain, ordinary people just like you and me.

As we read on in 1 Samuel 22, we see how David escaped from King Achish by portraying himself as something he wasn't, and he ended up in the cave of Adullam. David didn't realize that this cave was going to provide him a hiding place and a place of refuge and also a place of growth and training, and it would teach him to wait on the Lord. Here we see how David is likened unto Christ in his refusal to attack God's anointed so that he could be elevated to his rightful position.

I relate David's situation in the cave of Adullam to playing hide-and-seek in that when we think we are hiding to avoid confrontation, God may actually lead us to a place where He can allow us to grow the most. He can train us and teach us to wait on Him. When you decide to finally stop playing games in your daily walk with God, you will find, as I did, that God will begin to remove all distractions from your life. He may take all of your standards and expectations and kick them right out from under you. He may even take you to the most humble and loneliest place, where only you and He can know what is truly going on in your heart.

That was what was going on with Saul and David. Saul was sitting in the comforts of the palace, sitting on his high throne that once exalted him as king; but he was rejected of God, and he was refusing to surrender or submit to God. This unfortunately represents the way of the world, and sometimes our own hearts as Christians. We would sometimes rather be comfortable in this world, enjoying the passing pleasures of sin, in order to avoid the discomfort of just having it removed from us altogether. If we could just have the temporary blinders removed from our eyes to realize that it is keeping us from the will of God in our lives.

I believe that when we get to the place where we are tired of playing games with our walk with God, God will begin to separate us from all we have known to be "safe." As said before, He will begin to remove distractions from our lives; that could be bringing us out of our hiding places. When we look at David in this cave, we see that those who came to the cave, those he was captain over, were in trouble, in debt, or just discontented. How can you reach out to those in trouble, in debt, or discontented if you are right there in the midst of those issues yourself, or you've never been there to identify with them?

Jesus said in the Bible, "It is the sick who need a physician" (Mark 2:17). If you are not aware of your need, you won't be inclined to seek a cure. I believe that God had to get David to the cave of Adullam so that he could remove the distractions from his life and so that he could lead those who would be brought to the cave. David is a foreshadow of Christ, who would attract to Himself the hurting, the burdened, and the outcast. What kind of cave is God leading you to? What kind of distractions is He trying to remove from your life so that you will be able to minister to the hurting, the lonely, the downcast, or those who have been in the very same hiding places you are coming out of?

Words—Spiritual Containers

"We can make a large horse go wherever we want by means of a small bit in its mouth. And a small rudder makes a huge ship turn wherever the pilot chooses to go, even though the winds are strong. In the same way, the tongue is a small thing that makes grand speeches. But a tiny spark can set a great forest on fire. It is a whole world of wickedness, corrupting your entire body. It can set your whole life on fire, for it is set on fire by hell itself. People can tame all kinds of animals, birds, reptiles, and fish, but no one can tame the tongue. It is restless and evil, full of deadly poison. Sometimes it praises our Lord and Father, and sometimes it curses those who have been made in the image of God. So, blessing and cursing come pouring out of the same mouth. Surely, my bothers and sisters, this is not right. Does a spring of water bubble out with both fresh water and bitter water? Does a fig tree produce olives, or a grapevine produce figs? No, and you can't draw fresh water from a salty spring." (James 3:3-12)

Has there ever been a time in your life when you were having the best day that you could possibly have, all the world seemed bright and cheery, and you felt like everything was just as it should be? Then all of a sudden, out of nowhere, it happens. You are having a conversation with someone, they are having a bad day, and you just happen to be the victim of circumstance. Words are said to you, about you, and maybe right to your face. What happens? There goes your best day right down the tubes; you feel the countenance of your face change, and it seems as if all the air in your balloon just fizzles out, and you are left standing there holding the string. All because of words; they are like spiritual containers.

I like to relate the containment of our words to a bowl with a lid tightly sealed on it, like you would have in your kitchen. If you take something and put it in that bowl and put the lid on, it seals. If you drop that container or shake it, that seal will not be broken. It takes something of great force to break the seal to make the lid come off—our words are like that as well. When words are spoken over your life for a long period of time, they seem to contain you—they produce something of a spiritual seal over you that keeps you from moving forward. It takes something of great force and power—like the blood of Jesus Christ—to break the seal over your life.

I have heard it said that for every negative word spoken over your life, it takes twenty positive words to counteract it. Can you imagine how many positive words it would take to counteract forty years of negativity? God's Word is positive and cancels any negativity that the world may speak or pronounce over your life. I have found in my own personal studies that for every negative word someone has spoken over my life, I can find a Scripture to counteract and cancel it. For example, if someone says, "You will never amount to anything," God says in His Word, "For I know the plans I have for you, declares the Lord. They are plans for peace and not disaster, plans to give you a future filled with hope" (Jeremiah 29:11). With one Scripture, God lets us know that our future is in His hands, and He already has a good future set in motion for us, no matter what people may think about us.

When I was born, I was adopted on the very day I took my first breath. I later learned that I did stay a few days with my biological mother before being brought to the family that I know as "my family." I have to say right from the start that I am very thankful for the family that I have. God knew exactly what He was doing when He put me right where He did, so to my family, let me say, "I love every single one of you with all my heart."

If anyone reading this book has been adopted, you can identify with me that along with that comes a lot of baggage, a lot of places that you can hide. Places of insecurity, always wondering why you weren't loved enough so that you had to be given away, wondering if it will happen again; a low self-esteem, feelings of rejection … and the list seems to go on and on.

Once I found out that I was adopted, all those emotions began to sprout or take root in my life. By the time I was old enough to understand what those emotions were, that root had already grown from a seed and into a tree with deep roots. If you have ever cut down a tree, you know that sometimes the roots go way down deep. After chopping down the tree, sometimes you have to get a piece of machinery to help pull up the stump. The roots of the tree have grown down so far and so deep that it is impossible to remove the stump within your own power—an axe or a shovel—so you get a high-power piece of machinery. Sometimes you have to pray and fast, stay in the Word of God. God sometimes uses people in your life to help pull those "stumps" out of your life to get those deep roots out.

You see, at the very onset of my life through the adoption process, a seed of unforgiveness started without my even knowing it. Through words, that "seed" sank deep into my life, and I allowed it to take root. Throughout my life, it infiltrated every relationship I have ever had. I didn't know that until later in life when people tried to show me that, but at times I didn't care and didn't want to deal with it. Sometimes in your life, the people who care about you the most can tell you and tell you about something that is wrong in your life; you get so tired of hearing about it that you tune them out. I believe that is what I did.

In 2005, I lost the person I loved most in my life when my mother died because of health complications. I went through a time when I didn't want any more relationships in my life. I didn't think anyone else could love me like my mom did, and I didn't want to open myself up to love again from anyone. I became bitter, angry, and, yes, I hid behind my anger and bitterness. I even dared anyone to come and try to find me. I didn't want to be found. The place where you don't want to be found any longer is a very dangerous place to be. Words were controlling my life—ones that were spoken by people and ones that were spoken by the enemy of my soul. At this time, I was even speaking words over myself, and I didn't realize it. I didn't think that I could go on without my mother, and I was very lost. I felt like I had no identity and no purpose. I had almost convinced myself that without my mother, I couldn't go on and would be better off dead. The enemy of my soul was trying his best to convince me that all hope was lost. What he didn't realize was that my desperation was forcing me to look for the hope that my inner man was craving, the true hope in Jesus Christ that I was slowly turning my back on during this desperate time.

One day after enrolling in the mentoring institute, I heard a little clip of a television show on which two mentors of mine were talking about the difference between the truth and a lie. They were talking about how the Devil is a liar, the father of lies, and when he speaks there is no truth in him, and how he speaks his own language (John 8:44). After hearing that little clip of their show and really realizing what they were saying, it brought liberation to my heart and soul. No matter what the enemy says to me in my mind, it is only what He *thinks* of me, and it has nothing to do what God thinks of me, and what He says about me. People may say one thing about me, but what matters is what God says about me; because, after all, He is the one who created me.

There has been an individual in my life who continually told me I would never amount to anything, and that I was not worth anything to anyone. To everyone else, this person would say the opposite, but to my face, he would say the things that would bring me to tears. I knew what the Bible said about me, but I didn't really know how to combat what the enemy was telling me through this person whom I so desperately wanted to love and accept me. I couldn't understand why someone could say those things to me and then say something totally opposite to others about me. This person's words seemed to render me powerless, and I couldn't combat those words in my mind with what the Bible was telling me about myself. At times, I only had the Word in my head; it really hadn't made it into my heart. You see, that person was saying that I wasn't worth anything to anyone, and that I would never amount to anything; that is what the lies of the enemy said. The truth that God had spoken over me before I was even born was written in Jeremiah 29:11:

> "For I know the plans I have for you," says the Lord; "they are plans for good and not for disaster, to give you a future and a hope."

I also found out that in His Word, it also says in Psalm 139:13-17:

> You made all the delicate inner parts of my body and knit me together in my mother's womb. Thank you for making me so wonderfully complex. Your workmanship is marvelous— how well I know it. You watched me as I was being formed in utter seclusion, as I was woven together in the dark of the womb. You saw me before I was born. Every day of my life was recorded in your book. Every moment was

laid out before a single day had passed. How precious are your thoughts about me, O God. They cannot be numbered.

So the one thing I have learned about words: whether they come from people or from the enemy, you always have to combat the negative with the positive. A mentor once said to me, "Whatever you feed will become larger in your life." Meaning that if I constantly fed the negative, that would always be the most powerful voice in my life. It would always hold me captive and render me powerless. If I chose to combat the negative with the positive, then the positive would render the negative powerless, and therefore the containment of the words would finally be broken by the power of the name of Jesus Christ and by the power of the Word of God.

Whether people make fun of you for being fat, short, too skinny, freckle-faced, for wearing glasses, for where you come from, what nationality you are, it doesn't matter. Life and death is in the power of the tongue, and we have the power to choose to give life to people or to give them death. I had to choose to start combating the negative with the positive, to start gaining victory. So I have two questions to ask at the end of this chapter: Will you choose to come out of hiding and make the choice to no longer let negativity keep you from being all that God wants you to be? Are you giving life to people with your words, or are you constantly giving death with the poison of your tongue? Let's take just a moment here and reflect. What are some negative voices in your life that you may continually be listening to? What are they trying to convince you of? What part of your destiny are they keeping you from? Are you speaking life to those around you in your family, your job, your church? Take some time to reflect on these areas, and ask the Father to reveal to you ways that you can change your words to reflect His heart—not only for your life but for the life of those around you.

When we cause death to someone with our words, it is not a physical death, it is a death to their spirit—and it will take a divine intervention to revive that spirit that is slowly dying. I know because you are hearing from a person whose spirit has been given a death sentence many times. When there is a call on your life, and when prophetic words have been spoken over you, there is no enemy that can take you out before your time.

Defense Mechanisms and Fortified Walls

Just recently, I was in a conversation with a couple of friends, discussing some things that I had dealt with in my past, and the words "defense mechanism" came up. I was told in this conversation that I sometimes used my humor as a defense mechanism to avoid dealing with the real issue at hand or to avoid letting people get close to the real me, for fear of being hurt again or rejected. I had to sit back for a few minutes and really think about that one, but it was true; humor had become my way of taking the attention off the situation at hand and putting it somewhere else other than where it needed to be.

Defense mechanisms are those unconscious mental thoughts that we use to avoid anxiety, conflict, or any other problems or stress. In doing lots of research, I found that there are many different kinds of defense mechanisms that people use to hide from the reality of what is going on in their lives. In my own life, I was presented with the fact that I used humor to keep people from getting close to me. After evaluating that statement, I have found that it was and is true. I also found that I used sarcasm and self-deprecation as a way of keeping people out. You see, I thought that if I went ahead and made a wisecrack at myself, if I beat someone else to the punch, then I wouldn't have to hear someone else make the wisecrack, and it wouldn't hurt so much. Have you ever been there? Have you ever seen someone looking at you a certain way and known they were wanting to say something to you, so you just open your mouth before you think and make a wisecrack? Only to find that what they were thinking of saying was absolutely nothing like what you were thinking. In your mind, it was okay, though, because you saved yourself from a *potential* stab at your heart. This is not the way that you and I are created to live, with self-imposed anxiety.

Proverbs 12:25, ESV says:

> Anxiety in the heart weighs a man down,
> but a good word makes him glad.

First Corinthians 7:32a says:

> I want you to be free from anxieties.

First Peter 5:7 says:

> Cast ALL your anxieties on Him, because
> He cares for you.

God never intended for you or me to live underneath the weight on self-imposed anxieties, the curiosity of what people think of us or what they are going to do to us. The only thing that matters in this life is what God thinks about you and me. If we have the approval of the One who knew us before we were even formed in the womb, what more approval do we need in this life? So I ask you to take a small inventory of your life for a moment and see what defense mechanisms you might be using to keep people from getting to close to you. Examine those mechanisms you use when God wants to deal with issues you need to confront in your life. Is it anger? Humor? Denial? What is He speaking to you at this very moment? Listen—He is speaking.

Along with these defense mechanisms we use, we also develop fortified walls. These are walls we put up thinking that we are using them to protect ourselves, when in reality they are holding us captive from the very destiny that God has planned for us from the very beginning. What do I mean by *a fortified wall?* A fortified wall is anything built up (physically or emotionally) to withstand and prevent any kind of oncoming attack.

As we go through life, we try to defend ourselves against any type of attack (anger, rejection, verbal abuse, etc.). At first, we may not be successful with our defense. Over the years, we seem to learn what works and what doesn't, and that is how we develop those fortified walls. If something doesn't work to protect us from those oncoming attacks, we try something else, until eventually we become numb, and we search out other ways to protect ourselves from pain, rejection, or any other kind of harm.

One of my fortified walls has been my weight issue. A lot of women (and men too) have dealt with this issue at length, some to the point where they have become comfortable with it. When you become comfortable, that is when the walls start to become fortified and become a death trap.

As an example, until I left for college at age seventeen, I was a size twelve. When I went away to college, my "freshman fifteen" became my "freshman thirty." Within the next year or so, I developed a medical condition that required me to take a lot of medication that had many side effects. One was significant weight gain. I suffered many bouts of severe depression, and what do some women do when we are depressed? We eat. Long story short, over twenty-two years, my weight reached a high of 455 pounds, and it was a very unhealthy time in my life.

There were so many obstacles in my life at that time, and one was a very prominent person who was constantly at me because of my weight—my father. Out of respect, I will not share the things that he said to me, because I understand that he only wanted the best for his daughter; but I will say that these comments became a source of anger for me and became a layer of that fortified wall that caused me for many years to not really trust any men. I don't mean that just in terms of relationships, but in every way, even in friendships. Sure, I would hang out with my friends, and some of those friends were guys—but when it all came down to it, I had a few select friends who I would let get close to me and I would share my heart with. Truthfully, at that time, there was really only one person, and I trusted her with my entire life. So throughout those years, I developed a huge distrust because of all the weight jokes and wisecracks that people made. I guess they thought that making jokes and cutting me down would make me angry enough to lose weight, but it didn't. It made me angry all right, angry enough to shut down and say, "I am okay with myself, and when I am ready to deal with it, I will. Until then, leave me alone." When I said those words, I didn't realize that I was adding another layer to my fortified wall of bondage. This also became a source of my sarcasm as well, and sometimes without realizing it in conversations, that sarcasm would come out. I would end up hurting someone with my words without meaning to.

About two and a half years ago, I realized that God was calling me to do some things, and there was no way I could do them in the condition I was in. I was going to have to do something about my weight. I honestly didn't want to have to deal with this, because I had tried every diet on the planet, every weight-loss gimmick. You name it, I had done it, except gastric bypass and lap-band surgery. My weight became my excuse not to do what God was calling me to do. It became another "hiding place" for me—until that day I reached the 455-pound mark, and I knew it was time to try one last time. If I didn't succeed in losing some weight, I would be this way for the rest of my life. I did find a plan that worked for me, and I did lose a hundred pounds in a year's time. I wish that I could tell you that the weight jokes stopped and the cut-downs ended—but they did not. The one main figure in my life who I hoped would see a difference in me never saw a change. Even though there was a physical change and other people saw it, he did not. It was just recently that I was able to lay that part of my fortified wall down and let the Lord heal me from those scars. I am so thankful for the Scripture in 1 Samuel 16:7b that says:

> For the Lord sees not as a man sees: man looks on the outward appearance, but the Lord looks on the heart.

That is one of the layers of my fortified wall that the Lord is breaking through day by day. What layers is the fortified wall of your life made up of? Is that wall so strong that it seems nothing can break through the hard exterior of your heart and save you from yourself? Does you sometimes feel numb? Have you lost your tears? When was the last time you cried over something that you truly cared about? If that is how you feel, I have good news for you. The name of Jesus, and the power of the blood that He shed on the cross over two thousand years ago can break through any wall that has been built up in your life. His love can break through any hardened exterior of your heart, and He can actually give you a new heart, so you can feel again. As we continue to look on at some other things that we go through as we come out of hiding, I believe that you will start to feel a "cracking" of the fortified walls. By the time we get to the end of this book, it will be time for the walls to fall down. God loves you very much, and it is no coincidence that you picked up this book and that you are reading it at this very moment. Victory lies ahead for you.

The "Sting" of Self-Sabotage

When you hear the word "sabotage," what do you think of? I think of our military men and women first and foremost, because they have to think about how they can sabotage the plans of those they are fighting against to protect those they serve.

We can define the word sabotage as anything done to make things more difficult, or anything done to wreck something or to bring something to a state of ruin. So if we were to take this definition and add the word "self" to it, wouldn't the definition of "self-sabotage" read something like this: anything done by oneself to make things more difficult, or anything done by oneself to wreck something or to bring oneself to a state of ruin?

This is a very difficult chapter for me to write, because in reflecting back on my past, I can see many times when self-sabotage has kept me from reaching places I have desired to be. Someone might ask, Why would people do things to keep them from achieving success? There are several reasons; it could be fear of success and not knowing how to deal with that success, the feeling of not being worthy enough, the feeling of not being good enough to achieve that success. The list could go on and on.

In my own life, I have experienced the sting of self-sabotage because I didn't feel like I was worthy enough to have that kind of success, and I wasn't good enough. I know of two times that I was lined up for a very well-paying job as a nurse; one was in Virginia and another in West Virginia. Both were right out of nursing school. I didn't think I could handle the fast-paced life of a nurse in a hospital setting, and I didn't think I was good enough to work there, so I failed the pharmacology tests at both interviews on purpose. I know that it sounds silly, but when fear has a hold of your life in many different ways, it can cripple you at times and keep you from the very destiny of your life.

So what must we do to stop the vicious cycle of self-sabotage in our lives? *First* we must give ourselves over to the Lord on a daily basis, continually letting Him bring us through a process of realizing that we are good enough for anything He places in our path to do. Whether it is a job, a new ministry, a new friendship, no matter what it is, we are good enough. Of course, on our own, we aren't worthy of anything, but because of the blood that Jesus shed on the cross for your sins and mine, that is what makes us worthy. When we ask Him into our hearts and lives to become our Lord and Savior, to cleanse us from our sin and cover us in His blood, that is what makes us righteous and worthy, our commitment to Jesus Christ.

Secondly, we must make a personal commitment to self-discipline. We know what triggers the beginning of an act of self-sabotage. We feel the fear starting to grip our hearts; we feel the anxiety rising. It is during this time of anxiety and fear that we must start to pray and pick up the Word and find Scriptures to combat our fear. During this time, we must realize that we can't fight this alone. I encourage you to do as I have done. I have a small number of friends whom I call "confidants," people I call upon when

I am in those high times of anxiety and fear. They speak words of life to me and help me pray through. These are not just my everyday friends; these are a select few who have earned my trust and I know I can share the very depths of my heart with. They are the ones who will help me pray through those hard times.

Thirdly, I have found that if you aren't reading your Bible and praying on a daily basis, then when those hard times come, that is when your anxiety and fear will rise. If you are praying and reading the Word on a daily basis, then what you have been reading will arise within your spirit, and you will be reminded. You can then combat the enemy with what you have been learning from the Lord as you pray and as you read.

I have also found that our poor choices can create a crisis that we never expect to face. That could involve purchasing a car, knowing that we cannot afford to make the payments, which later results in our being in debt or even having to file a bankruptcy. It could be the choice of using the credit card instead of using the money in our pocket, just because we can pay it off later. We get in the rut of doing that, only to realize a month later that we have maxed out our credit card and the interest is about to drive us crazy and we are now struggling with another payment to make. If only we had used the money we had in our pocket, or if we could have just done without. Maybe it's knowing that the Bible tells us as believers not to be yoked together with unbelievers, but yet we just can't let go of that man or woman who keeps coming around and paying us attention, or who we have dated before and the Lord has specifically told us "no." It could be so many different things.

The key is to soak it in prayer and to listen for the voice of the Lord in every situation. Never make any decisions based on your emotions. This gets so many people in trouble. We must always base all of our decisions on the Word of God and the leading of the Lord and the Holy Spirit. Sometimes you may even need to do some fasting along with your praying about the situation. I am learning more and more that when faced with a tough decision, if I do not have peace about what I am getting ready to do, then I'd better not do anything until I have peace in my heart and spirit. God is not the author of confusion; He is the author of peace.

As we operate in this little game of self-sabotage, we may not realize that we use "defense mechanisms" to protect ourselves. So many people use defense mechanisms to avoid having to deal with reality, and this in itself is a form of self-sabotage. Some people use alcohol, drugs, promiscuity, sarcasm, humor, anger, and so much more to cover up the deep wounds that lie beneath the surface of their lives. As a means of protection, they resort to one of these defense mechanisms to protect themselves from being hurt any worse than they already have been. Have you ever seen an animal that has been hurt? What does it do when you approach it? It takes that area of its body that has been hurt and turns it away from you or it protects it with another part of its body. That animal may even growl at you or snap at you.

We, as Christians, must learn to stop playing the game of self-sabotage. It does have a nasty sting to it, and sometimes we don't feel the sting until later on in life, somewhere down the road. Just remember that every choice you make in life has a consequence, either good or bad. We must make a conscious effort to make those good choices in life.

And now, dear brothers and sisters, one final thing. Fix your thoughts on what is true, and honorable, and right, and pure, and lovely, and admirable. Think about things that are excellent and worthy of praise.

(Philippians 4:8, NLT)

To Fear or Not to Fear, That Is the Question!

"For God has not given us a spirit of fear, but of power and of love, and a sound mind." (2 Tim. 1:7)

In doing research on fear, I found it noted that in the Bible, the phrase "do not fear" is mentioned 365 times. Isn't it so awesome that the God who loves us so much would make that one phrase mentioned the exact number times as the same number of days in our calendar year? That is one "do not fear" for every single day of your life.

There have been many situations in my life that have left me crippled by fear, agitation, and anxiety, leaving me full of dread. I have heard it said that fear is "False Evidence Appearing Real." In court, in order to win a case, a lawyer must present evidence that his or her client is not guilty. The prosecutor must present evidence that the one being charged is guilty. With no concrete evidence, there is no case. The evidence for fear is just that; it is false when it comes to Jesus. The Bible tells us plainly that "perfect love casts out all fear" in 1 John 4:18. We know that there is only one who is perfect, and that is Christ Himself. The Bible tells us plainly that "God is love" in 1 John 4:8b. So if perfection and love come together in the form of Christ, and He casts out all fear, then it is up to us to combat our fear with faith. Another mentor in my life gave out an acronym for faith one day, and it has been something I have had to remind myself of when I get scared or fearful—"Fear Ain't In This House." I once heard a pastor say that "Fear knocked on the door, faith answered; and fear was no longer there."

I used to be afraid of so many things, and I still have things that I am working on; by no means have I arrived yet. I have stated before that I am a nurse, and as difficult as it is for me to admit, until this year I was very afraid of needles. I could give anyone a shot, and if there was a major emergency, I would jump in and be ready to save a life. But let someone come at me to take my blood, give me a shot, or let me cut myself and need stitches, I was so gripped with fear that I would pass out. It was a great fear for me. Many of you know what I mean when I say that fear would render me powerless. There is a story in my life that no one has ever known until this year that caused me to be so fearful of needles.

In my late teenage years, I went through a major period of depression. I was eighteen years old when I attempted suicide for the first time, and I say *the first time* because there were other times that no one else in my family knew about. After spending some time in the hospital and then coming home, there were weeks when I felt very alone and scared. Everyone knew what happened, no matter what kind of story I made up to cover what I had done. Even though there were people who I knew loved and cared about me, I was in my own little world at that time, trying to deal with my own life. I had heard about people who were "cutters," who used knives and other sharp objects to cut themselves, to release the pain and anguish that they were feeling. But at that time, I didn't want to have scars or cuts all over me; so what did I do? I would take needles and stick myself in the arms, sometimes in the legs with them; they looked like bug bites, so no one ever questioned them. This went on for about seven months after the suicide attempt, and I started going to college after that, so I had something else to occupy my mind. Later on, though, when I had to go to the doctor for a shot or to have blood drawn, it would throw me back to that time when I used to do that to myself, and I would begin to panic. The enemy used that time to create a stronghold in my life without me even seeing it or realizing what I was allowing him to do. I was going to church at that time, but I was taking some time off from all the things I was doing, other than going to college. I thought I was okay. This stronghold in my life was a fear created by myself, but turned against me, ultimately meant to hold me captive from my destiny.

In December 2010, I moved from Virginia to Cleveland, Tennessee, and right about mid-January, I started having a lot of issues with bronchitis and borderline pneumonia. When I lived in Virginia, it was normal for me to get bronchitis about twice a year because of the cold temperatures in the winter and then the humidity in the summer. I had only been in Tennessee for two months, and in early

February, I made my first trip to the emergency room for a fever that would not stop and being unable to breathe. Come late March, I was getting ready to take a cruise, and I was determined to not go on this cruise sick. A mentor friend of mine said, "You need to go get a shot and get better." Well, I went into a frenzy. I whined around in my fear until it got to the point where I was fighting just to breathe, and I had to face my fear and go for a shot. That isn't saying that I was happy and I went in there with smiles on my face; I was scared to death. There comes a time in your life when you just have to confront what is staring you in the face and tackle it head-on. I got the shot, and guess what? I didn't pass out; in fact, I didn't even feel it. I was so overwhelmed in the stronghold of fear that I couldn't see what God was doing in making me face my fear. Now, I am not saying that God made me sick just to make me face my fear. I am saying that He used what the enemy meant for evil, and He turned it around for my good.

I have known for a long time that missions is a part of my calling in life—not long term but short term. If you know anything about missionary work, you know what you have to get before you can go overseas—shots. Sometimes more than one shot is involved, depending on where you are going. So in facing that fear, not only did I break the stronghold that had been holding me back, but I felt like I made some progress toward an area of my calling. Since that time, I have been on a mission trip to Ireland, and I plan to go on as many short-term mission trips as the Lord allows me to.

I believe that when you close the doors to strongholds that have been holding you captive in your life, God will begin to open doors that you never even dreamed possible, even doors that you never dreamed. Jeremiah 33:3 says, "Call to me, and I will answer thee; and show you great and mighty things, which you know not of."

There are other areas of fear that I have faced in my life, but another thing that has brought me freedom is learning the meaning of my name. For a long time, I was referred to as, "Lake and Tina's daughter" or "one of the Cox children." Now, don't get me wrong; there is nothing wrong with being known by your parents or being known by your last name. The Bible says that a good name is to be chosen rather than riches, but sometimes you just want to be known by your first name; know what

I mean? For my fortieth birthday, a friend of mine looked up the meaning of my first name on the Internet and gave it to me as a gift. I have always found when I looked up my name, "Terri," that it meant "tenderhearted." In some places, when you look it up, it does mean that; but it is a secondary meaning. The actual meanings of my name are these: Leader of the Tribe, Harvester, Bold, Capable, Authority, and Strength. This is the opposite of the name I have always heard.

Being a nurse, you have to learn how to be tenderhearted toward your patients, and yet you also have to learn how to be tough, because in some situations as a nurse, people will misuse your tenderheartedness to their advantage. I am tenderhearted, and I have a hard time saying no; that sometimes that gets me in trouble. I think that for the longest time, I tried to live up to my name—the one that was a secondary definition—and it caused me to move into what Joyce Meyer calls "approval addiction." Some of you can probably relate to trying so hard to please people that it puts you into a place of fear. Although I didn't see it as approval addiction, I have been the type of person who wanted to make things better for everyone else, and it didn't matter if what I needed or wanted ever got taken care of. As long as others were happy, I felt like I was doing what I needed to be doing. For a long time, when people would call me into an office at work, and even in church, my first response was—"Whatever I did, I am sorry; and whatever I didn't do, I apologize, and I will go do it right now." Approval addiction in action, right? Yes, it is. As humans, we want to please people, but sometimes in wanting that, it can become such a way of life that it becomes a hiding place for us. If we are always doing what is needed to get people's approval, then we don't have to worry about being hurt or rejected. Once you get into that "hiding place," you are fearful of telling people no, and you make yourself vulnerable to being taken advantage of by others. I have gotten to this place in a lot of relationships. In not being able to say no, I kept myself under so much unnecessary stress and anguish. That is what happens when we look to others before we look to God for approval. We must realize that God's approval is already ours, and it is worth more than anything else we will ever need. "For thou, Lord, will bless the righteous; with favor will thou compass him as with a shield" (Psalm 5:12). When our hearts finally learn that God's approval is all we need, we will learn that sometimes we can be so busy *doing things* for the kingdom that we are missing out on what we are *really* supposed to be doing. Approval addiction can be traumatic in the long run; it is a stronghold that needs to be broken, just like any other fear. The blood of Jesus, along with the power of the Word and His name, can break any stronghold that has power over your life.

Changing Your Perspective

Have you ever gone on vacation somewhere, and then a few years later gone back and it seemed like nothing was the same as it was before? There could be various reasons: the place is no longer owned by the same people, and the new owners have changed things around; you are a few years older than you were the last time you were there, and maybe you don't remember exactly the way things were last time; maybe your perspective has changed since the last time you were there.

When I was little, we used to go to Disney World every year. I loved going on the ride called, "It's a Small World." I remember sitting on the little boat and riding around, seeing all the places that represented different countries, and I remember hearing the song that played—"It's a small world after all. It's a small, small world." As I got older, I realized that it is not such a small world after all; it is a great big world, and it can be overwhelming at times. Sometimes we get so overwhelmed with things, the perspective we once had as a little child becomes tainted and marred. I remember a pastor giving an illustration about our problems using a quarter and a piece of paper. As he was preaching, he held up the quarter and said, "Let this quarter represent your problems, and then let this piece of paper represent God." (If I remember correctly, he was using an index-card-sized piece of paper.) Then he said, "God isn't very much bigger than the size of your problems, is He? Kind of makes you doubt a little bit, doesn't it?" Then he dropped the quarter on the carpeted floor and he said, "If this entire carpeted area represented God, then what does that do to the size of your problems?" He paused and waited for a few seconds and said, "The size of your God changed the perspective of your problems, didn't it?" Sometimes to get to the next level of our destiny, all we need is a perspective change; that may mean a new job, a move to a new city, a new school/college; it may mean different things to different people.

In February of 2010, I began to feel a deep stirring in my spirit that a huge change was coming to my life; but at that time, I wasn't quite sure what it was. As I began to pray, I began to sense that God was going to move me away from everything I knew to be "comfortable and safe." He was going to take me completely out of my comfort zone and into something brand-spanking new. How exciting, and yet scary at the same time.

At the end of February, I felt the Lord speak to me about starting to apply for nursing jobs. I started applying for them in the town I lived in, and in a couple of surrounding towns not more than fifteen to twenty minutes away. After three months of applying for jobs, I began to apply for out-of-state jobs in Tennessee. It was so unlike me to do that, because I was the kind of girl who never saw herself actually leaving the confines of her hometown or her home church. I thought that I would be there forever, eventually find a husband, have at least one child, and be with my family and friends until Jesus came back. However, I started applying for out-of-state jobs in May, and I must have applied for at least thirty-five nursing jobs and been turned down for every single one. Rejection after rejection, turndown after turndown; I was getting flustered, but I knew that something had to turn up soon. Finally in September, I got called to go to Cleveland, Tennessee, for an interview. So I went, and nothing ever came of it. Rejection again. One day, I remember being in my car, and I was very angry. I was tired of being turned down for job after job after job. I remember stopping on the side of the road and telling God, "I know that You have told me that something new is headed my way, and I feel like a move is coming; but I won't go until there is a job and a place to live, and I have to get a release from You to go. I feel so miserable, Lord. Please do something or take this stirring away; I can't stand it!" Like I have said earlier, I have never been pregnant, but some women have told me that there comes a time when a pregnant lady gets so uncomfortable that she cannot sit still, she can't lie down—she just gets so uncomfortable that she is miserable. In the spirit, I believe that is where I was. I was believing and praying for what I was feeling inside my spirit, and I was waiting for it to be manifested. I was waiting to see it with my own eyes. Romans 4:17 says to "Call those things which be not, as though they were," so I started to call that job in. I began to pray and remind the Lord that if I was to move to Tennessee, the right job needed to come along and also the right place to live. This went on for another month.

In November, I got a phone call to go for an interview with another company. They asked me to fax them a resume, and I could fill out an application once I got there for an interview. I loaded up the car and headed to Tennessee. If I remember correctly, I had a meeting the night before the interview; my friends agreed with me that if this was the job that God had for me that it would just fall right into place. I walked into that interview the next morning (or at least what I was told was supposed to be an interview), and it turned out to be an orientation with the company; and before I walked out the door I was already filling out my tax papers, going for a drug test, and a hepatitis B shot. The funny part is that I still had not filled out the application yet, and I was due to come back to start work in three weeks. After leaving there, I was supposed to go look at two places that were for rent. When I drove onto the property at the first place, my spirit said "No." I didn't even go and look at the place; I drove right off the property and went to the next place. Within the next hour, I not only had a job, but I also had a two-bedroom apartment that would be ready when I came back in three weeks, and I didn't even know that four of my friends lived in the same complex. As I drove back to the office of the mentoring institute that afternoon to see some friends, I was in complete awe of what God had done in a matter of five hours. My entire life was about to change completely. The question became, was I ready to take the next step into transition? I did, and I have seen God move in so many mighty ways ever since. I have seen some doors open that I never even dreamed of seeing open since I took that step of faith.

My big perspective change in moving to Tennessee is that I have had to learn to trust God more than ever before. When I was back in Virginia, I had the security of having my family and all my friends around. It was a safe place for me to hide. Being in a new town, in a new job, it was just me and God. Yes, I have friends here in Cleveland, Tennessee, and I have an awesome, huge church family. But here I cannot hide in the same hiding places I used to, behind the things or people I used to hide behind, because they are not here with me. It is okay to want to be with family and friends and to think that maybe you are supposed to stay right there with them in life, love, and ministry until Jesus comes. In my case, though, when you have a desire to reach the world, you have to change your perspective to reach beyond your home community and beyond where you have come from. Sometimes you can only make so much of a change where you are, and God will move you to a new place where He can teach you something new, or change your perspective. He may have bigger plans for you than what you have even thought of. Sometimes we just dream too small. Jeremiah 33:3 tells us that He will show us the great and mighty things that we know not of—if we will call unto Him. Do you feel that deep stirring in your heart and in your spirit that something *big* is coming your way? It may be a move to another state or a ministry change or even something that you don't have the complete picture of yet; you may just have a small glimpse of what it may be. I encourage you to pray and seek God's face until you have that release to move or until He gives you that "witty invention," or until you have that new ministry idea or business plan. You can never go wrong in soaking something in prayer and having the mind of Christ in all things. I can relate this to having a baby once again. When a mother carries a baby, and it is born prematurely, it has a hard time breathing on its own and often has to be in an incubator for a period of time. There might be other complications as well. When God is birthing something in you, you don't want to jump into it prematurely before its time. If you jump before its time, there will be problems and chaos, and it will be a premature spiritual birth, meaning "before its time." Birth pains are just that, painful; but when the time is right and the birthing is over, mothers will tell you that the pain is worth it all. Hang on if you are feeling those "birth pains," because the pain will be worth the wait. His timing is perfect.

There are some little perspective changes that I am still working on, and the process hurts; but gain without pain is no gain at all. There is an old country song that Barbara Mandrell used to sing called, "I Was Country When Country Wasn't Cool," and I think that song used to be my excuse. "I'm just country and don't know no better." What I am learning is that when you begin to move forward, your perspective has to move forward with you. You never forget where you come from, you never forget your roots or your foundation, but you never let it become your excuse for not moving forward. Being country used to be my excuse for hiding some of the talents God has given me. In reality, I was just afraid that what I had was not good enough. It has taken some good friends to keep reminding me that I am not what people said I was; but I am what God says that I am. Second Corinthians 5:17 says, "Therefore if any man be in Christ; he is a new creature; old things are passed away, behold, all things are become new." So sometimes all we need is a new perspective, and like I said, changing your perspective may mean just finding out how God wants you to look at a situation. Stop looking at it through your eyes, and look at it through His eyes. It may mean a move for you to a new city, to a new church; it may mean a new job. It is never the same thing for two people. So, how is your perspective today? Do you need to have your spiritual eyes examined by the Great Optometrist? Sometimes our eyes become cloudy, and our vision becomes unclear of what God has planned for us, and we have to ask God to open the eyes of our heart. Take time today to stop and reflect; then pray and ask

God to open the eyes of your heart and reveal your current perspective to you and ways that you might need to make some changes. Ask Him to help you to make those positive changes today, and watch Him go to work on your behalf.

Coming Out of Hiding Takes Courage

"Have I not commanded you? Be strong and
courageous. Do not be frightened, and do
not be dismayed, for the Lord your God is
with you wherever you go."
(Joshua 1:9, ESV)

The very title of this chapter can be very scary, and
it can make you shudder. Just as an animal who has
been hurt has to learn to trust again, coming out
of our hiding places takes great courage. First of
all, we must come to the realization that our hiding
places were really not protecting us at all. They were
really fortresses of confinement, keeping us from

our destiny that we could have been attaining all along.

We have got to come to the place in our lives where we desire true freedom in the Lord more than anything else. True freedom in the Lord doesn't mean that we aren't going to be hurt ever again or that we aren't going to be rejected or people aren't going to make fun of us anymore. It just means that the Lord is going to help us find ways to deal with those issues as we face them, and instead of going into hiding, we are going to learn to praise our way through it.

I was in church one day with a precious little girl named Jadynn Allen. I remember she got up and talked to us about praise being a weapon. She was quite correct when she spoke that powerful word that day. Our praise is just like a weapon in our hands, and when we praise from our innermost being, it cuts the enemy. You see, he was the worship leader in heaven until the day he fell. When we break out in true worship and praise, it reminds him of where he was and where he still could have been today, had he not gotten all selfish and tried to make himself bigger than God. So again, when we praise God with all our heart, not only does it remind him of his past, but I also think it reminds him of his future.

When you start to come out of your hiding places, people will start to notice a change in you, and some are not going to understand. Where you used to be angry about some things and full of sarcasm, the Lord is going to help you to replace that with love, mercy, and grace. Where you used to hide behind your weight because you were afraid the Lord might call you to the mission field, you might find that He will call you to a ninety-day challenge and give you the plan just for you to help you lose that weight you so desire to lose. When those people who used to make fun of your weight and cut you down throw those comments at you, you will find that your response will start to be different. Where you used to walk away in tears and become depressed, you might find that you will walk away and begin to pray for them. Our pastor sings a song called, "I Feel a Change," and I guarantee that when you start to come out of hiding, you will start to feel that change coming on … and you will love it. The one thing that you *must* remember, though, is that you have to lean on the Lord and trust Him through the process, because it will not be easy, and you will want to go back into hiding. If you trust Him fully, and those He leads you to be accountable to—He will bring you out of hiding and into true freedom in Him.

"Where the spirit of the Lord is, there is freedom."

2 Corinthians 3:17

"Trust in the Lord with all your heart, lean not on your own understanding; in all your ways acknowledge Him, and He will make your paths straight."

Proverbs 3:5-6

Whatever it Takes

I remember a story told to me not long ago about a little girl who was playing hide-and-seek with her father, and they had been playing for about ten minutes. Now, we all know that when daddies play with their little girls—the game is a little different than if it were a bunch of nine- and ten-year-olds playing outside in the backyard. Of course, the daddy is counting, "Seven, eight, nine, ten. Ready or not, here I come." The little girl has run and hidden where she *thinks* Daddy doesn't know where she is, but all along, Daddy can see her little pink shoes sticking out from under the curtains that cover the front window in the TV room. As he is "looking" for his little girl, he looks under the table, in the laundry basket, and everywhere else possible—except where he knows she is hiding, all because he loves her and he wants her to win, to get back to home base before he finds her. All of a sudden, he hears out of her frustration, because she wants to be found, "Daddy, here I am. Come find me."

My life had come to this point in 2008. In fact, it had come to a complete standstill. I had come to the place in my relationship with God where I was saying, "There has to be more to serving You than this, because if this is all there is, then I am missing something." So I began to search for whatever I was missing. I had no idea what it was; I just knew that there had to be something more than what I was experiencing at that stage of my life.

Have you ever been so thirsty that nothing else will quench your thirst but a *huge* glass of ice water? You can drink a glass of tea, soda, lemonade, or whatever might be in the refrigerator, but nothing will satisfy you like a huge glass of water. That is where I was, searching for a huge dose of whatever the Father had for me; but I didn't know what He was leading me to at that point. The point is, I was so desperate, I was willing to do anything to get it. *Sometimes you have to let desperation get behind the wheel and drive you to your destiny.* I began to look on the Internet, but to be honest, I didn't know what I was looking for. I just went surfing.

One day, I came across a video for the International Institute of Mentoring in Cleveland, Tennessee, and as I watched this video, something inside my spirit "jumped" and caught me off guard. The only way I can explain that feeling is if you have ever been pregnant and you have felt your baby "quicken" within your womb—the first time that the baby actually moved and you felt it. I have never been pregnant, but I am a nurse, and I have been with people who were pregnant, and they have tried to explain that to me. In the spirit, I now know what they were describing. Let me say, I am not writing a book about the mentoring institute, but I have to mention it to explain my process of how I played this game of hide-and-seek, so that you can see how God has brought me out into the open. So I saw this video in November of 2008, and I looked to apply to the mentoring institute, but their Main Event for that year had already passed, so I made plans to go the next year. I knew something was drawing me there, or rather, I knew God was drawing me there for the next level, for which He was preparing me.

In 2009, I sent in my application for the mentoring institute, and I was headed to the Main Event in October of that year. I had never been to Cleveland, Tennessee and didn't even know that there was a Cleveland, other than the one in Ohio. A week before I left to attend the Main Event, I started to get nervous. For one thing, I was going all by myself, and I didn't know a soul there. A friend of mine told me that it was a good thing not to know anyone, because no one knew you, so it was like a fresh, new start. A couple days before it was time to leave, I had already talked myself out of going, and I had come up with every kind of excuse that you could think of to not go. I was running to my hiding place of comfort. I knew once I stepped into this new realm that God was going to require some things of me, and I was starting to wonder what He was actually setting me up to do. A friend of mine looked at me one day in my living room and said, "You are going, and that is that." She really didn't say it exactly like that, but you have to understand, I can sometimes be a little stubborn and bull-headed, and you just have to lay it all on the line to me. I am very glad she handed me a little dose of tough love that day. I knew that I needed to go, because I was searching for something

I needed in order to survive. Everything we need to survive is all wrapped up in Jesus Christ. Of course we need air, water, food, clothing, shelter, and all those necessities to survive physically; but spiritually we cannot make it in this life without Jesus. When our spirit is starved and we need that "something more" and we get desperate, that is when we go searching. Proverbs 8:17 (NLT) says:

> "I love all who love me, those who search will surely find me."

Ezekiel 34:16 (NLT) says, "I will search for my lost ones who strayed away, and I will bring them safely home again. I will bandage the injured and strengthen the weak."

Isaiah 55:6 (NLT) says, "Seek the Lord while you can find Him, call on Him now while He is near."

I believe that is what I began to do on this journey; I was so dry and desperate for a move of God in my life that I had to get to a place where I had to have something more. I didn't know that once I started on this journey, He was getting ready to take me on the ride of my life.

Once I got to the mentoring institute in Cleveland, I was very scared and unsure of what I was about to walk into, let alone what I was about to experience. What I found was a place full of passion, a place dedicated to serving and mentoring those who have a call of God on their lives; a place full of people who opened their hearts and arms to me and said, "We're ready to mentor you and help you achieve your goals and ultimately see God catapult you into your destiny." I knew I had found what I was looking for. Sometimes you need a place to go where you can be restored, renewed, and revived. I can look back over the last two years and say that God has led me to a process of restoration, renewal, and personal revival. I haven't totally arrived to all that God has for me, but He is healing me from the inside out. When I say that, I feel that I need to explain myself a little. Have you ever cut yourself and tried to heal it on your own? You put Neosporin on it, a Band-Aid, and eventually it does heal up, and sometimes you have a scar. When you look back and see that scar, you remember the exact time and place when that injury happened, don't you? I am a nurse, and sometimes when there is a deep wound, you have to clean out the bacteria. Instead of putting stitches or staples in it, sometimes you put packing material in the wound to let it heal from the inside out. Most of the time when that happens, there is no scar to remind of that injury. In my life, there have been some instances that have left some scars, because I have tried to fix things on my own. But God in the last two years has been taking me on a journey of healing—from the inside out, and the scars are slowly disappearing. I am learning how to forgive. Forgiveness brings about a healing that modern medicine has yet to discover. Scars may be a sign of healing, but if healing can come without a scar, it's a sign of not only healing but wholeness through Jesus Christ.

Ready or Not, Here I Come

Believe it or not, we are not the first people to play hide-and-seek with God. Adam and Eve were the first people to play hide-and-seek after they ate of the forbidden fruit. They realized they were naked, and they hid in the garden when they heard the Lord walking in the cool of the day. They hid so well that in Genesis 3:9, the Lord actually says to Adam, "Where art thou?" We even get to see a little of the "blame game" taking place in this chapter as well—Adam blames Eve, and then Eve turns around and blames the serpent, and all three end up being cursed.

Think about the story of Jonah. He was called to go to Nineveh, a place where he did not want to go. He refused and instead went in the opposite direction. He wound up on a boat and was cast into the sea and then swallowed by a great fish. In Jonah chapter two, Jonah prayed to the Lord out of the fish's belly, and the Lord heard his voice. These are just a couple of the people who played hide-and-seek in the Bible; there are plenty more. These people thought they were playing hide-and-seek, but He had already turned it around, and they didn't realize it. In my own case of playing hide-and-seek, there were times when God asked me to do things that I didn't want to do, and I ran in the opposite direction and wound up miserable, just like Jonah did. Had I just gone where God had asked me to, life would have been so much simpler at that time. There is no place more aggravating to me than to be miserable because you have been disobedient to God's leading. You can't be comfortable in anything because every day, and it seems like every minute, something reminds you of your disobedience. You get more miserable as the days go on, until you just can't stand it anymore and you finally give in and do what you should have done from the start. Some people call that stubbornness, and I have been guilty of that. To this day, I still have my moments of being stubborn and wanting my own way. We have to surrender our lives to His process daily. We have all been guilty of playing the blame game, just like Adam and Eve did. A husband says, "Well, if my wife wasn't such a nag, maybe I would think about doing ..." Then you hear, "Well, if my husband would be a little more considerate, I might just ..." Come on now, we have all done it. As a single person, I have said, "Well, if so-and-so hadn't said that to me, then I wouldn't be so afraid of commitment." We all could create our lists, but the truth of the matter is that we all need to grow up and take responsibility for our own actions and our own games of hide-and-seek.

We must talk about God's alternative to our game of hide-and-seek, and I believe it is called "seek me and be found by me." He is always revealing things to us, but I think that we are so often looking for the "big" things that we miss the little things like His still, small voice, the morning sun as it falls on your face as you wake up, or the sound of the waves crashing on the shore in the early morning hours.

Deuteronomy 4:29 says:

> "If from thence thou shalt seek the Lord thy God, thou shalt find Him, if thou seek him with all thy heart and with all thy soul."

Psalm 63:1 says:

"O God, thou art my God; early will I seek thee: my soul thirsts for thee, my flesh longs for thee in a dry and thirsty land, where no water is."

Isaiah 55:6 reads:

"Seek ye the Lord while He may be found, call ye upon Him while He is near."

There are other Scriptures that could be put in with these three, but you see where I am going with this. The Father is always seeking us as we are in our hiding places. He is longing to bring us out of those places so He can take us into the new places of destiny that He has waiting for us. The key is that we have to be willing, and we have to trust Him.

Proverbs 3:5-6 (NLT) says:

"Trust in the Lord with all your heart, and lean not unto your own understanding. In all your ways acknowledge Him, and He shall direct your path."

It is hard, but we have to be willing like the little girl in the story near the beginning of the book, and we have to say, "Daddy, here I am; come find me." Have you come to the place where you are so tired of hiding behind all the excuses as to why you can't do and be all that you are called to be? Are you tired of all the hiding places that you thought were protecting you and keeping you safe? Do you now realize they have only gotten you more entangled in the snare of the enemy that tightens chains of life tighter around your hands, feet, and neck? Well I have news: He is ready to come running to your rescue. All you have to do is ask Him—and if you ask for it, you will get it. The freedom that awaits you when you come out of your hiding places is very liberating. It almost feels as if a thousand pounds of weight is lifted from your shoulders. Relieve the stress of trying to impress people or having their approval any longer. Just knowing that as long as the Father gives His seal of approval over your life, it is the most liberating thing that can ever take place in your life, it breaks the chains that have held you captive for so long. I know that when this revelation came into my heart and soul, it began a process of setting my life free, and I started on a journey of freedom that I never knew existed.

Matthew 7:7-8 (KJV) says:

> "Ask and it shall be given to you, seek and ye shall find, knock and it shall be opened unto you. For everyone that asketh receiveth, and he that seeketh findeth; and to him that knocketh it shall be opened."

It is no secret that we are living in what is called the "last days." There are wars and rumors of wars, earthquakes, tornadoes, famines, and so much more that is going on. The signs are all point to His imminent return, and we must live our lives like today could be the very last day we have to live. You see, God is coming back for a church, a body of believers that is without spot or wrinkle—without blemish. And just like in the game of hide-and-seek, when the Father tells Jesus that it is time … Jesus is going to be saying, "Ready or not, here I come." Therefore, we must always make sure that our heart is right before the Lord, and we are ready to go when He comes. We do not know when He will come; the Word says that He will come as a "thief in the night." I don't know about you, but I want to be ready. I don't want to be left behind here when all the chaos begins. It is time we quit playing games with God, so at this point I must ask a pertinent question. Are you ready should He come back before you finish reading this book? Have you surrendered your life to Jesus Christ and accepted Him as your personal Lord and Savior? If you have not, I must give you the opportunity to do that at this time. God loves you very much, and He gave His one and only Son as a sacrifice for our sins. There is no one who can and will ever love you like He does, and the Bible even says in John 15:13, "greater love hath no man than this, than a man lays down his life for His friends." That is exactly what Jesus did for you and me. We are not promised tomorrow; in fact, we are not even promised our next breath. We need to make sure of where we are going to spend eternity, with or without Jesus. So if you would like to take some time right now to give your life over to Jesus and accept Him into your heart, just simply pray this prayer:

> "Jesus, I come to You today realizing that I
> cannot live my life on my own. I cannot make
> it without You. I ask You today to come into
> my heart, cleanse me of every sin that separates
> me from You. Wash me clean in the precious
> blood that You shed on the cross for my sin,
> and make me brand new in You. Come and

be the Lord of my life, and help me to live my life every day as You would have me to live it. Thank You for forgiving me, and for loving me so much that you came and died for me. I choose You today, and I accept You into my life and leave the old life behind. I choose to follow You, and to serve You from this day forward. In Jesus' name, Amen."

If you prayed that prayer, my friend, then you have now accepted Jesus into your heart, and you have now started a new life in Christ. I would encourage you to get a Bible (if you don't already own one) and start reading it every day, and start attending a good Bible-believing church with good praise and worship music. Get involved and start listening for the voice of God as He begins to lead and guide you in this new life of yours as a Christian.

If you have already accepted Jesus as your Savior prior to reading this book, then my statement to you is that it is time for the church to rise up and "be the church." Amen? If we, the church, continue to stay in our hiding places, then we continue to put wrinkles in the train of the "bridal gown" of the body of Christ. He as called each of us to a specific work, to a specific destiny, and He has nothing but good plans and a good future for us, as pointed out earlier in this book. We just have to stop letting fear, intimidation, words, a cloudy perspective, and self-sabotage keep us from pressing forward into that place that God has waiting for us. If we stay in hiding, are we truly pursuing the heart of God for our lives? Are we really surrendering our all to the One who gave His all for you and me? One day, God will speak to Jesus and let Him know that it is time for Him to come and get His bride, and we will be hearing Jesus say to us, "Ready or not, here I come." I believe the Father is saying to us individually and also as a corporate body, "Come out, come out wherever you are." I know that He is waiting with open arms; there is healing, deliverance, and whatever else you need right there with Him. Freedom is yours for the asking, and yours for the taking.

Come Out, Come Out, Wherever You Are

The good news in reading about the people like Jonah, Adam and Eve, that played "hide-and-seek," is that they were all found by God. The Bible talks about how in the last days, the enemy would go around and try to deceive the very elect, if possible (Matthew 24:24). I know that in my life, the enemy tried his very best to deceive me by keeping me in places of hiding and also by letting me think that I was protecting myself safely in those hiding places. He wanted to convince me that it was all right to keep myself from being hurt again or rejected, that it was my right to hide. Let's face it: we are going to be hurt in this life; it is just going to happen. But we have a friend that sticks closer than a brother

(Proverbs 18:24), and in Hebrews 13:5-6 it says, "I will never leave thee, nor forsake thee; so that we may boldly say, The Lord is my helper, and I will not fear what man shall do unto me."

The Lord is able to speak to you right where you are, right in those hiding places that the enemy is using to keep you from your destiny. If the desire to stop playing hide-and-seek has overtaken you and you are ready to be found by the true seeker of your soul, it is my prayer that in sharing some aspects of my game of hide-and-seek, you can see how you can enjoy so much more of this life than what you are experiencing. He wants to give freedom to you now.

My journey has taken me almost three years to start coming out of my hiding places. It has not been an easy process, but He is helping me and healing me from the inside out. He can do the same thing for you. God is no respecter of persons, and He loves us all unconditionally.

Not everyone is ready to give up their comfort zones or their hiding places, but when you become so miserable or so desperate for a change in life, you will let your desperation get behind the wheel and drive you to whatever changes need to be made to make a difference. Perhaps some of you have come to that place in your life where you are tired of hiding behind excuses, you are tired of being intimidated, you are tired of needing the approval or acceptance of everyone else to feel like you have some kind of self-worth. Is that you? If that is you, then I would encourage you to take the time to pray this prayer:

Dear Jesus,

I thank You for allowing me to pick up this book and learn more about the comfort zones in my life, and those places of hiding that are keeping me from the destiny that You have designed and destined for my life. Please send Your Holy Spirit to come and overshadow me and to seal every word that has been sent to my heart as I have been reading. I know that in playing games with You, I have been placing myself in great danger, in danger of being lukewarm in my relationship with You. I ask You to forgive me right now for playing games. At times I may have been playing games unknowingly, and yet at times I have been playing those games on purpose because of circumstances and situations in my past that

I have been holding on to. I repent and ask forgiveness for holding on to my past, and I say today *the past is just that, the past.* No longer can I change what has happened back then. I can change what happens from this moment on, and I choose to come out of hiding, and to be found by You, the true Seeker of my soul. Begin to reveal to me any other areas of my life that need to be worked on, because I am a work in progress, and I want to move forward into the destiny that You have designed for me from the very start. Thank You for loving me as I am, and for loving me enough to challenge me to be better than what I am at this point in my life. I love You, Lord, and I thank You for who You are, and for Your ultimate sacrifice that You paid. Today is a new day, and I step into victory and into true freedom, and I am being found by You every day. In Jesus' name, amen.

Do you hear that? I hear it . . . listen . . . it is faint . . . but it is getting louder . . . listen . . .

"Come out, come out . . . wherever you are . . .

Ready or not . . . here I come."